Fishing with Dad

Fishing with Dad

Michael J. Rosen
Photographs by Will Shively

ARTISAN
NEW YORK

Most every Sunday,
when I was little,
my father took me
fishing.

I remember it all,
especially now,
watching another boy
at his side. . . .

We're up before the sun—sometimes, we're off even before the doughnut shop is open and we have to wait a few minutes for breakfast. "But that's when the fish are biting," my Dad says, "and that's when we're out fishing." Every Sunday.

Second stop is Harry and Dot's for bait: nightcrawlers (in a cottage cheese container!) and a sack of squishy, licorice-flavored doughball. Then it's country roads and gravel roads and dirt roads and a hike through a farmer's field.

(Dad knows directions to anywhere), until . . . we're here, our fishing hole! "And no one else has found our spot!" Dad says. We have it all to ourselves—not to keep, just to borrow till after lunch. So then we unpack the gear:

a cooler of soda and sandwiches (for later), three fishing rods (it's hard to keep them from tangling!), folding stools (they're *my* size, not Dad's!), a net that's taller than Dad, our holding bucket (for watching the fish before we let them go), and Dad's amazing tacklebox (with drawers that open out like a fishing stadium that's stocked with everything— even a snake-bite kit, though we've never even seen a snake). Dad puts on his favorite fishing vest

(it's got eleven big and little pockets), and we
take turns wearing the greenish hat with all the lures
at the band that Dad has had since he was a boy—
it's still too big for me. For my rod, I pick a bobber
that's red and white,

two pea-sized sinker weights, and the wiggliest worm that won't stop squiggling into letter shapes. "Maybe the fish can read, and it'll spell B E W A R E," I say to Dad. At last, we're ready. My dad casts two poles, I cast one; sometimes,

I cast into the trees. "Fishing for birds?" Dad asks. Unsnarling the hook takes a while. Finally, all three bobbers are floating offshore, and we set the poles in the forks of three sticks. What's left is just the being patient part.

Dad's an expert at that, too; not me. Going fishing is really going waiting . . . with a little bit of fishing thrown in. But Dad says, "That's the relaxing part." He *likes* relaxing! But I like *fishing*—you know, *catching fish!*

We're quiet so we don't scare off the fish. We're watchful, because some sly fish or shy fish will steal your bait if you're not paying attention. (They'll nibble the worm and never bite the hook!) And . . . we're also bored; at least I am.

Dad says watch for the bobber to jiggle or dip or zip across the water, but almost always it's just the current wiggling it. Or Dad says watch the tip of the rod to see if it wobbles or bounces or bends, but mostly it just points

to the clouds or treetops. I'm *not* fishing
for birds! Or Dad says gently pinch the line and feel if
it quivers or twitches or twangs, but a little breeze will
make it do that, too. All the lines and bobbers and pole
tips do is wait—with us.

That's when I organize the tacklebox. The rubber worms and buggy-looking bobbers and the bug-eyed jigs and painted spoons and plugs, all the poppers and spinners and feathery crawlers (I'm careful of hooks)—they all need separate compartments.

When I'm done sorting, if the bobbers haven't dipped and the poles haven't bent and the three lines haven't twitched, and the fish haven't bitten, I ask if maybe I can go skip stones . . . a ways away so I won't scare the fish.

I can skip a stone ten times sometimes (not usually) while I'm waiting for Dad, who's waiting for the bobbers, that are waiting for Dad, who's waiting for the bobbers, that are waiting for the bait, that are waiting for the fish . . . but he hasn't called, "Quick, we've got one!" Not yet.

Searching for skipping stones, I usually find: a hairy caterpillar, a milkweed pod with a million, trillion wishes for me to make, seagull feathers and fossils dotted with shells, and something lost from someone's tacklebox.

"Come on back and watch the poles," Dad calls, even before I run out of stones to skip. "Give me a chance to stretch the old legs." So I plop down on the folding stool and watch three poles, three lines, three bobbers, all doing

their usual nothing on this beautiful Sunday morning that Dad says is why we're really out here anyway—like we've come to catch a beautiful Sunday morning instead of a fish. But then, all on my own, one of the lines

whines a high *eeeee* . . . and I feel it slide between my fingers. The bobber dunks, then zips, unzips! zigzags across the waves, and the fishing pole—I grab it just in time—doesn't just bounce, it bows down and points to the water, as if to say *Right here! Here!* is where the fish is! But where is Dad? "Quick, we've got one, Dad!" I yell, reeling and reeling until I hear him next to me. He scoops the net into the splashing water—

look!

it's a large, flipping, largemouth bass, a chubby catfish, or a flopping colossal perch. "How'd you do that?" he asks. "I've been waiting all morning, and look who pulls out the first fish!" But, really, I don't know how. Dad's the expert.

He grips the slippery fish in his wet hand and frees the hook. "There's your prize fish," he says, and slides it into our holding bucket so I can see up close the fins rippling open and closed, the gills beating open and closed—even the jaws open and close. A few minutes later, we let the fish go, and it's waiting time again for our second catch . . . but the bobbers just bob, and the poles point up at—hey, turkey vultures are circling the creek!—

but the line feels just like a string on my guitar at home, except the stupid fish aren't strumming. Pretty soon, I take another walk. If Dad catches the second or third fish, I race back to see what kind and how big,

and if it accidentally swallowed the hook, and if Dad has to use the needle-nosed pliers. Later, Dad wants to stretch his legs again. My turn to watch. I give up collecting or skipping and wait for a fish to nibble or steal the worm

OR *something*—but it's amazing: I hardly wait at all and I've got a bite! The line twangs and zips, and the pole dips toward the bobber (which dove underwater!)—it happens all at once. "Dad, it's another one!" I yell. "But bigger!"

And then more things happen all at once: me reeling and Dad netting and a tail flopping into the bucket. "Well, how'd you find him!" Dad asks. (Big ones are always "him.") "I've been waiting half the day for him,

and just like that you pulled him out! Good catch! I'm proud of you." But I don't know how, really. Dad's the expert. Some days we catch a dozen fish before it's too hot and too bright and the fish stop biting. Sometimes, two or three.

But that's not counting the hundred skipping stones, the trillion milkweed wishes, all the rock and fossil and feather collecting, the waiting and waiting, and the lot of Sunday morning we've caught before we pack up the tackle and head back.

Now I'm the age
Dad was when he first took me fishing, and
there's another boy who wears his too-big, greenish
fishing hat (that fits me now) and calls my father Zee—
that's short for *Zayde*—that's Yiddish for grandpa.

So now my father shows this boy exactly how to bait
and how to cast and, of course, how to be patient, too.
But when the boy gets tired of going waiting, he
wanders off, and *I* see the fishing secret my father kept

all these years and never showed me—not once: He
catches a fish, reels it gently to shore, secures the hook
so that it won't slip free, and lets the line out so the
fish can swim away. And when he calls the boy to come
and watch

so he can stretch his even older legs, one of the bobbers and the line and the pole perform their fishy magic then and there, without the briefest wait, in front of the little boy's eyes, in the middle of a beautiful Sunday morning.

And it's a chubby catfish, a large—or even a smallish—largemouth bass, or a flopping perch, and it's Zee, my father, who's saying, "How'd you catch him? I've been waiting all summer for this guy!" And now, I know how. My dad's the expert.

For my father, Marvin Rosen, who was the inspiration as well as the model—
along with his grandson Benjamin Rosen—for this book.—MJR

For the many people whose kindness and generosity have inspired such joy in this creation,
particularly Michael, the kids, and Michael.—WS

Michael J. Rosen is the author or editor of some sixty books for adults and children, including *Dog People*, *Horse People*, and the best-selling *Kid's Book of Fishing*. He lives in central Ohio.

Published by Artisan
A Division of Workman Publishing, Inc.
708 Broadway, New York, New York 10003-9555
www.artisanbooks.com

Library of Congress Cataloging-in-Publication Data

Rosen, Michael J., 1954–
Fishing with dad / story by Michael J. Rosen; photographs by Will Shively
ISBN 1-57965-286-7
1. Fishing—Fiction. 2. Fathers and sons—Fiction. 3. Grandfathers—Fiction.
I. Shively, Will, ill. II. Title.
PZ7.R71868Fi 1996
[E]—dc20   95-43892   AC

Printed in China

First edition 2005

10 9 8 7 6 5 4 3 2 1

Book design by Jennifer S. Hong; redesigned by Nicholas Caruso